HAL•LEONARD
INSTRUMENTAL
PLAY-ALONG

AUDIO
ACCESS
INCLUDED

PLAYBACK+
Speed • Pitch • Balance • Loop

# TROMBONE

# CHRISTMAS CLASSICS

| | |
|---|---|
| Angels We Have Heard on High | 2 |
| Bring a Torch, Jeannette, Isabella | 3 |
| Coventry Carol | 4 |
| Fum, Fum, Fum | 5 |
| Go, Tell It on the Mountain | 6 |
| God Rest Ye Merry, Gentlemen | 7 |
| Here We Come A-Caroling | 8 |
| The Holly and the Ivy | 9 |
| I Saw Three Ships | 10 |
| Jingle Bells | 11 |
| O Come, All Ye Faithful | 12 |
| O Holy Night | 13 |
| Silent Night | 14 |
| Still, Still, Still | 15 |
| What Child Is This? | 16 |

Audio arrangements by Peter Deneff

To access audio visit:
**www.halleonard.com/mylibrary**

Enter Code
7894-3262-1421-6244

ISBN 978-1-4950-7060-0

HAL•LEONARD®
CORPORATION
7777 W. BLUEMOUND RD. P.O. BOX 13819 MILWAUKEE, WI 53213

In Australia Contact:
**Hal Leonard Australia Pty. Ltd.**
4 Lentara Court
Cheltenham, Victoria, 3192 Australia
Email: ausadmin@halleonard.com.au

Visit Hal Leonard Online at
**www.halleonard.com**

# ANGELS WE HAVE HEARD ON HIGH

TROMBONE

Traditional French Carol

# BRING A TORCH, JEANNETTE, ISABELLA

TROMBONE

17th Century French Provençal Carol

# COVENTRY CAROL

TROMBONE

Traditional English Melody

# FUM, FUM, FUM

TROMBONE

Traditional Catalonian Carol

# GO, TELL IT ON THE MOUNTAIN

TROMBONE

African-American Spiritual

# GOD REST YE MERRY, GENTLEMEN

TROMBONE

Traditional English Carol

# HERE WE COME A-CAROLING

TROMBONE

Traditional

# THE HOLLY AND THE IVY

TROMBONE

18th Century English Carol

# I SAW THREE SHIPS

TROMBONE

Traditional English Carol

# JINGLE BELLS

TROMBONE

Words and Music by
J. PIERPONT

# O COME, ALL YE FAITHFUL

TROMBONE

Music by JOHN FRANCIS WADE

# O HOLY NIGHT

TROMBONE

French Words by PLACIDE CAPPEAU
English Words by JOHN S. DWIGHT
Music by ADOLPHE ADAM

# SILENT NIGHT

TROMBONE

Words by JOSEPH MOHR
Music by FRANZ X. GRUBER

# STILL, STILL, STILL

TROMBONE

Salzburg Melody, c.1819

# WHAT CHILD IS THIS?

TROMBONE

16th Century English Melody